D0674986

SPOT 50
Horses &
Ponies

Camilla de la Bedoyere

Miles
KeLLy

First published in 2010 by Miles Kelly Publishing Ltd
Harding's Barn, Bardfield End Green, Thaxted, Essex, CM6 3PX, UK

Copyright © Miles Kelly Publishing Ltd 2010

This edition printed in 2011

2 4 6 8 10 9 7 5 3

Editorial Director Belinda Gallagher

Art Director Jo Cowan

Editor Sarah Parkin

Image Manager Liberty Newton

Production Manager Elizabeth Collins

Reprographics Stephan Davis, Jennifer Hunt, Ian Paulyn

Assets Lorraine King, Cathy Miles

All rights reserved. No part of this publication may be reproduced,
stored in a retrieval system, or transmitted by any means, electronic,
mechanical, photocopying, recording or otherwise, without the
prior permission of the copyright holder.

ISBN 978-1-84810-251-4

Printed in China

British Library Cataloguing-in-Publication Data
A catalogue record for this book is available from the British Library

ACKNOWLEDGEMENTS
All photographs courtesy of Bob Langrish excluding:
Page 4(br) Miles Kelly Publishing; 23 Timo Jaakonaho/Rex Features; 34 Miles Kelly Publishing

All artwork is from the Miles Kelly Artwork Bank

Made with paper from a sustainable forest

www.mileskelly.net info@mileskelly.net

www.factsforprojects.com

Self-publish your
children's book

buddingpress.co.uk

CONTENTS

Tick the circles when you have spotted the breeds.

TYPES OF HORSE

Horses and ponies are fascinating animals. They can be graceful, gentle and tame, yet incredibly strong and full of energy. Learning about these wonderful animals can be the beginning of a journey that grows into a lifetime of discovery.

Hotbloods
These are the fastest runners and are often used for racing. They are high-spirited and can be difficult to handle.

Arab

Coldbloods
These calm, gentle horses are large and strong. They were used for pulling heavy loads and farm work. Coldbloods are also known as heavy horses or draught horses.

Shires

Warmbloods
Warmblood horses were bred by crossing hotbloods with the large, heavy coldbloods of northern Europe. They are good runners, but are sturdier and calmer than hotbloods.

Camargues

What's the difference between horses and ponies?
The main difference is that ponies are usually smaller than horses. They also have shorter legs and may have long, feathery fur around their hooves. Their tails and manes are often thicker than horses. Many types of pony are known for their calm, patient natures. Falabellas are the smallest breed of pony standing around just 32 inches tall.

Arabian horse

Falabella pony

POINTS OF A HORSE

The parts of a horse's or pony's body that you can see have been given names, called 'points'. Some are similar to those we use to name our own body parts, but others are different. The points are useful when talking about the appearance of horses and ponies, how to look after them and how to ride, so it is useful to learn the points and where they are.

Poll

Ear

Forelock

Mane

Eye

Nostril

Hindquarters

Withers

Dock

Croup

Back

Muzzle

Shoulder

Chest

Knee

Cannon bone

Stifle

Tail

Thigh

Elbow

Pastern

Hock

Fetlock

Hoof

Measuring height

The height of a horse or pony is measured from the ground to the base of its neck (withers).

When people first began measuring the heights of horses and ponies they used their hands as units of measurement. A 'hand' – the width of an average man's hand – is four inches, or 10 centimetres. If the animal measures more than an exact number of hands, the extra measurement is given in inches after a decimal point. A height of 12 hands and one inch is written as 12.1 hh (hands high). Measuring a horse's height is difficult because many are taller than people. Horses and ponies also like to flick and twitch their heads!

AKHAL-TEKE

Known for its beautiful, metallic coat, the **classic Akhal-Teke is a hotblood that is both resilient and powerful.** These horses were originally bred in the deserts of Turkmenistan, Central Asia, and they cope well with the intense heat of the desert and the scarcity of food and water. Akhal-Tekes are naturally athletic. Today, they are ridden in long-distance races, as well as dressage and showjumping.

HEIGHT
14.3–16 hh

In 1935, the strength and power of Akhal-Tekes was proved when Turkish horsemen rode a group for 4000 kilometres in just 84 days.

FACT FILE

Place of origin Turkmenistan

Colour Metallic gold, bay, grey, chestnut, black or palomino

Uses Long-distance racing, showjumping, dressage

Characteristics Courageous and strong

Long ears

Mane may be sparse or even absent

Long neck is carried high

Long back

Elegant head

Thin tail

Slender body

Long legs

Hocks are high set

Small hooves

ANGLO-ARAB

The Anglo-Arab is a cross between the Arab, giving it elegance and strength, and the Thoroughbred, giving it speed and intelligence. Anglo-Arabs are especially popular in France where they are bred for use in general riding and competitions. Although they are slightly smaller than Thoroughbreds, Anglo-Arabs have long legs, making them ideal for showjumping. They are also often used in the game of polo.

HEIGHT
15.2–16.3 hh

Anglo–Arabs are popular horses for endurance racing. During races they may cover distances of up to 80 kilometres a day.

FACT FILE

Place of origin England

Colour Chestnut, brown, bay or grey

Uses Riding, showjumping, dressage, long-distance racing

Characteristics Intelligent and fast

Long neck

Prominent withers

Strong hindquarters

Head has the look of an Arab

Body is deep through the girth

Long legs

Strong, well-shaped hooves

ARAB

Arabian horses are one of the oldest known breeds. Arabs are beautiful, clever and gentle, and are especially valued for the their speed and stamina. These horses have unusually short bodies because their spines have fewer bones than in other breeds. Arabs are high-spirited, but they handle well, making them popular with riders. Because of their genetic purity, Arabs have been used for centuries to improve and refine many other breeds around the world.

HEIGHT
14.2–15 hh +

The first Arabian horses were probably bred at least 1400 years ago. Most types of modern horse have Arabian bloodlines.

FACT FILE

Place of origin Arabian peninsula

Colour Grey, chestnut or bay. Brown or black is rare

Uses Riding, racing, showing

Characteristics Intelligent and high-spirited

Small head with large eyes

Silky mane and tail

Small muzzle

The angle at which the head meets the neck in Arabs is called the Mitbah

Short back

Tail is carried high

Body is deep through the girth

Flat knees

8

BARB

No one knows exactly when the first Barb horses appeared, but it is thought they developed after North African wild horses bred with Arabs or Akhal-Tekes. Barbs are strong and have good stamina, although they lack the elegance of other hotbloods. The Barb is one of the world's most ancient breeds. It has been used to breed other types of modern horse, but their numbers as a pure breed are falling.

HEIGHT
13.3–14.1 hh

The Abaco Barb is an endangered strain of the breed that lives on the island of Abaco in the Bahamas. The horses were shipwrecked there 500 years ago.

FACT FILE

Place of origin North Africa
Colour Bay, brown or grey
Uses Riding, racing
Characteristics Strong and tough

Large head

High withers

Sloping hindquarters

Tail held low

Upright shoulders

Body is deep through the girth

Short legs

Small hooves

THOROUGHBRED

Thoroughbreds have been bred for their impressive speed. They are the fastest horses in the world and widely regarded as the finest riding horses. Thoroughbreds are extremely intelligent and are quick to learn and respond to commands. They were first bred in England 300 years ago by mating three Arab stallions with English mares. Thoroughbreds are crossed with other breeds to improve them.

HEIGHT
15.2–16.2 hh

All Thoroughbreds can be traced back to one of three stallions used to start the breed — the Darley Arabian, the Godolphin Arabian and the Byerly Turk.

FACT FILE

Place of origin England

Colour Solid colours, such as brown, bay, chestnut and grey

Uses Riding, racing, showing, dressage

Characteristics Athletic and high-spirited

Long neck

High withers

Short back

Muscular hindquarters

Face may have white markings

Long, sloping shoulders

Long legs

Lower legs may have white markings

BOULONNAIS

According to legend, these coldbloods were bred from horses brought to France by Roman general Julius Caesar as he prepared to invade Britain in the first century BC. Boulonnais horses are strong, but they also have elegance from their Arab ancestors. In the 17th century, they were used to carry loads of fish over 300 kilometres from the coast to markets in Paris. These popular horses are still bred in parts of northern France.

HEIGHT
15.3–16.3 hh

The Boulonnais is usually grey, but breeders are now trying to introduce black horses back into the breed. This colour was common 200 years ago.

FACT FILE

Place of origin France

Colour Usually grey. Other colours are rare

Uses Farm work, pulling

Characteristics Calm and strong

Small ears

Elegant head

Muscular, curved neck

Straight back

Fine coat

Well-opened nostrils

Wide chest

Powerful shoulders

Legs have less feather than in other draught breeds

BRETON

Also known as **Draught Bretons, this is an old breed that goes back to the Middle Ages.** Bretons were developed in France to carry out heavy farm work, but they were also used to pull carts and during times of war. These coldbloods are quite small for draught horses, but they have a comfortable gait that made them popular with soldiers.

HEIGHT
14.3–16.3 hh

Bretons are famous for their ability to work in difficult conditions over long periods of time.

FACT FILE

Place of origin Brittany, France

Colour Chestnut, bay, grey, red, roan blue

Uses Farming, pulling

Characteristics Pleasant and friendly

Large head with a straight profile

Large, heavy body

Short, thick neck

Short, muscular legs

Small feet

CLYDESDALE

Clydesdales have been bred in Scotland since the 17th century. Native horses were crossed with larger stallions from Europe to develop this heavier, stronger breed. Clydesdales were originally used to pull ploughs and many were sent to Australia and New Zealand in the 1800s to work on farms. They were also used for pulling heavy guns and transporting supplies in France during World War I (1914–1918). As tractors became more common, Clydesdale numbers dropped.

HEIGHT
17 hh

Before a Clydesdale foal can be registered as a pedigree, a sample of its hair is sent for testing to prove its parents were both Clydesdales.

FACT FILE

Place of origin Scotland

Colour Brown, bay, black or roan

Uses Showing, pulling

Characteristics Quiet and strong

Broad forehead

Head has straight profile

High withers

Muscular hindquarters

Bay and brown with white markings are most common

Body is deep through the girth

Large hooves

Silky feathers around feet

DUTCH DRAUGHT

The heavy clay soils in parts of Holland made pulling ploughs tough work for all but the strongest horses. To solve this problem, farmers bred Dutch Draught horses, which are the heaviest of all coldbloods. They are strong and sure-footed, and are known for their quiet, patient temperaments. Despite their size, Dutch Draughts can move in a sprightly, energetic way. It is rare for these coldbloods to work on farms today, but they are often seen in show rings, pulling carriages.

HEIGHT
16–17 hh

The long-lived Dutch Draught is famous for its ability to work in tough environments for long stretches of time.

FACT FILE

Place of origin Holland

Colour Chestnut, roan, bay, black or grey

Uses Showing, pulling

Characteristics Powerful and calm

Short, muscular neck

Steeply sloping hindquarters

Short, muscular legs

Large head with a straight profile

Wide, muscular chest

Solidly built body

Highly feathered legs

FRIESIAN

Unusually elegant coldbloods, Friesians have delicate, attractive faces and quite long legs. However they have deep, strong bodies and are very powerful. They have been used in the past for farm work, and even carried Knights of the Crusades in the Middle Ages. Today, Friesians are still used for pulling carriages, especially during funerals.

HEIGHT
15–16 hh

Friesians make attractive carriage horses due to their black coats, thick manes, tails and feathers, and quick, high-stepping trot.

FACT FILE

Place of origin The Netherlands
Colour Black
Uses Driving, riding
Characteristics Sensitive and willing

Short ears

Sloping quarters

Low-set tail

A fine head and bright, alert face

Compact body that is strong

Long legs with feathers

NORIKER

Draught horses carry or pull heavy loads, and Norikers have been bred to haul heavy loads in steep mountain areas. As a result, this breed is sure-footed, hardy, reliable and with a good sense of balance. Norikers, which were once known as Pinzgauer Norikers, have been around for many years. Their numbers dropped when farmers replaced them with machinery, but they are still bred in the Austrian countryside.

HEIGHT
16–17 hh

Ancestors of Norikers were used to transport goods across the Alps before Roman times.

FACT FILE

Place of origin Austria

Colour Black, brown, chestnut

Uses Draught work, especially farming

Characteristics Calm and steady

Long mane and tail – often blonde or flaxen (pale yellow) in colour

Long back

Wide nostrils

Strong leg joints

Large girth

Few feathers

PERCHERON

These coldblood horses get their name from the region in northern France where they were first developed – **La Perche.** Percherons originate from local horses being bred with Arabs brought to France by invaders in the eighth century AD. Adding Arab blood to the breed produced powerful horses with good movement and an elegant appearance. Percherons have little or no feathering, which means their legs stay clean while working in the fields.

HEIGHT
16.1–17.1 hh

One of the world's tallest horses was a Percheron called Dr Le Gear. He was born in 1902 and his adult height was 21 hh — around 2.13 metres.

FACT FILE

Place of origin Northern France

Colour Grey or black

Uses Farm work, pulling, showing

Characteristics Elegant and hard-working

Broad forehead

Thick mane

Large eyes

Sloping hindquarters

Fine coat

Sloping shoulders

Body is deep through the girth

Short, powerful legs

Little or no feathers

SHIRE

The beautiful Shire is one of the most famous coldbloods. These tall horses were developed to work on farms, at docks and to help with the building of the railways. Their history goes back to Medieval times, when powerful horses were needed to carry soldiers in heavy suits of armour into battle. Shire horse numbers declined as tractors became common during the last century. They are seen at British agricultural fairs and shows, but they are exported around the world.

HEIGHT
16.2–17.2 hh

The Shire is named after the English counties, such as Cambridgeshire, Derbyshire, Leicestershire and Lincolnshire, where it worked on farms.

FACT FILE

Place of origin England

Colour Brown, bay, black or grey

Uses Farm work, pulling, showing

Characteristics Powerful and friendly

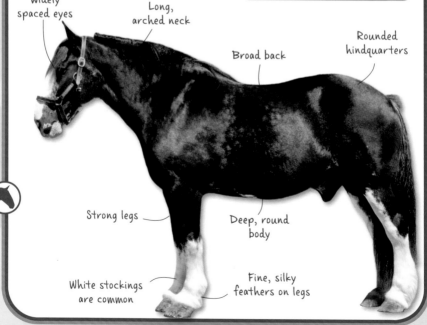

Widely spaced eyes

Long, arched neck

Broad back

Rounded hindquarters

Strong legs

Deep, round body

White stockings are common

Fine, silky feathers on legs

SUFFOLK

The Suffolk, also known as the Suffolk Punch, has had a difficult history. It was first bred around 500 years ago for agricultural work. The breed became particularly popular for its ability to work for long hours on little food. Numbers declined when machines took over the tasks they traditionally performed on the farm. New breeders have helped to save the Suffolk, but these horses are still rare and make welcome appearances at shows.

HEIGHT
16–17 hh

Every Suffolk alive today shares a common ancestor — a stallion called Crisp's Horse of Ufford, which was born in 1768.

FACT FILE

Place of origin Suffolk, England

Colour Chestnut, sometimes with white markings on face

Uses Farm work, showing

Characteristics Gentle and tough

Star, blaze or other marks may be visible on face

Thick neck

Low withers

Coat is always chestnut

Wide chest

Short legs

Stocky body

No markings or feathers on legs

19

AMERICAN SADDLEBRED

American Saddlebreds have become a popular breed because they combine great beauty with intelligence and adaptability. With their high-held heads, arching necks and expressive eyes, these horses are particularly popular in the show ring. They lift their legs high, and can perform two extra gaits in addition to the walk, trot and canter. The rack is fast and sprightly while the slow-gait is a prancing motion.

HEIGHT
15–16 hh

American Saddlebreds are mostly show horses, but they can also be used for general riding.

FACT FILE

Place of origin Kentucky, USA

Colour Chestnut, brown, black or bay

Uses Showing, driving, riding

Characteristics Calm and sensitive

Eyes are spaced far apart

Flat croup

Head is held very high and is well shaped

Very long tail

Deep and sloping shoulders

ANDALUCIAN

This breed is known for its elegant looks and long mane. Andalucians are intelligent warmbloods – they learn quickly and respond well to riders. This breed descended from wild Spanish horses and has been used to develop most modern horse breeds, including Lipizzaners, Connemaras and Welsh Cobs. In the 1700s, the breed nearly died out following a period of famine and plague in Europe.

HEIGHT
15–16.2 hh

Andalucians are one of the oldest breeds. They originate from ancient horses that are depicted in prehistoric cave paintings in Spain.

FACT FILE

Place of origin Southern Spain

Colour Mostly grey. Bay and black are rare

Uses Riding, dressage, driving

Characteristics Agile and calm

Large head with big eyes

Long, thick mane

Rounded withers

Tail is set low

Large nostrils

Broad, muscular chest

Muscular body

Strong legs with flat bones and large joints

Compact hooves

APPALOOSA

Bred from Quarter Horses, this breed is particularly strong and good-natured. In the 1700s, American Indians developed the breed by mixing their own native horses with spotted Spanish horses that were introduced to America in the 1600s. The American Indians favoured spots and patches of colour, which led to a variety of coat patterns. Appaloosas were kept as work horses but now they are developed for showjumping and dressage.

HEIGHT
14.2–15.2 hh

In some countries, the Appaloosa is recognized as a colour variety, but not a pure breed. In the USA they are a registered breed.

FACT FILE

Place of origin Washington, USA

Colour Spotted coats of varying colours

Uses Riding, showjumping, showing, dressage

Characteristics Athletic and versatile

White ring visible around the iris

Short, thin mane and tail

The body is coloured but the back and hindquarters are white with coloured spots

Mottled skin around the nose

Sloping shoulders

Hooves are often stripy

CAMARGUE

Camargues are now bred as riding horses, but for a long time they lived wild in southern France. Surviving in the wild meant that these small horses developed toughness and strength. Despite their size, Camargues can carry the weight of an adult with ease, and are used to round up wild bulls for bullfights. They were tamed by the Romans and were probably bred with European horses to develop other modern breeds, such as the Criollo.

HEIGHT
13–14 hh

Camargues are black or brown at birth. White hairs gradually grow through their dark coats and by their fourth year, Camargues are completely white, or grey.

FACT FILE

Place of origin Camargue region of France

Colour Grey

Uses Cattle herding

Characteristics Tough and courageous

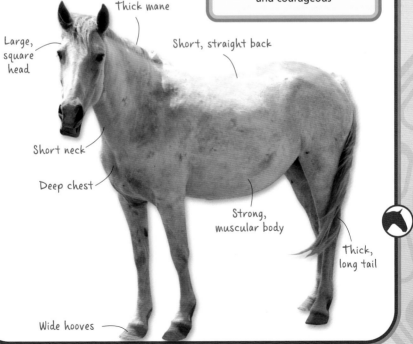

Thick mane

Large, square head

Short, straight back

Short neck

Deep chest

Strong, muscular body

Thick, long tail

Wide hooves

CLEVELAND BAY

Cleveland Bays have gentle natures. They have been bred in Britain since the Middle Ages, mostly in northern England. Admired for their elegant step and good nature, these warmbloods were popular carriage horses and are still used to pull royal carriages today. Cleveland Bays were used during World War I (1914–1918) to pull guns and were able to work for many hours before tiring.

HEIGHT
15.3–16.2 hh

The Cleveland Bay is the rarest and oldest of British breeds. It is crossed with other breeds, so pure breds have almost disappeared.

FACT FILE

Place of origin England
Colour Bay
Uses Riding, driving
Characteristics Intelligent and bold

White star may be present on forehead

Points (mane, tail, ear edges and lower legs) are black

Powerful hindquarters

Large head

Strong shoulders

Wide, deep body

No feathers on legs

CRIOLLO

Criollos are sometimes classed as ponies, because they can be below 14.2 hh and have pony-like bodies. They were bred from Spanish horses that were taken to South America to work with large herds of cattle. They are now regarded as one of the toughest breeds in the world, with incredible levels of endurance. They can take part in long distance racing, including events that continue for a week or more.

HEIGHT
14–15 hh

Criollos are not only strong, they are willing and intelligent, making them a popular breed.

FACT FILE

Place of origin Argentina
Colour Dun
Uses Driving cattle, racing
Characteristics Long-living and strong

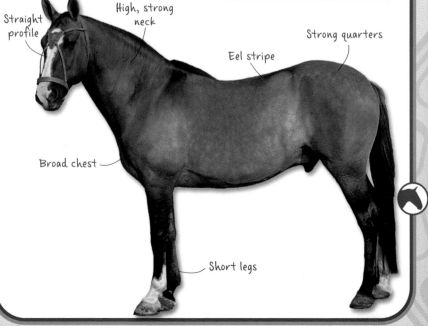

Straight profile

High, strong neck

Eel stripe

Strong quarters

Broad chest

Short legs

DUTCH WARMBLOOD

The Dutch Warmblood is one of the world's youngest breeds. It was developed in the 1960s by breeding Dutch horses with English Thoroughbreds. They have been bred for competitions, such as dressage and showjumping, and are one of the most successful competition breeds ever produced. Most have coats of a solid colour, but white markings on the legs and head are common.

HEIGHT
15.3–16.3 hh

Dutch Warmbloods are extremely fit, strong and resistant to health problems due to careful breeding.

FACT FILE

Place of origin The Netherlands

Colour Black, brown, bay, chestnut or grey

Uses Showjumping, dressage

Characteristics Tough and long-lived

Attractive face

Strong hindquarters

Tail is set high

Long neck

Sloping shoulders

Body is in good proportion

Strong, long legs with large bones

GELDERLANDER

Gelderlanders may not be beautiful, but they are tough. They were originally bred from a range of European horses for heavy farm work and to pull carriages, and they are still used for driving as well as riding. This breed is very adaptable, owing to its strength and gentle personality. Most Gelderlanders are chestnut in colour, with white markings, although grey horses also exist.

HEIGHT
15.2–16.2 hh

Gelderlanders are sometimes called multi-purpose horses because they are adaptable and suit new riders, as well as those more experienced.

FACT FILE

Place of origin Netherlands
Colour Chestnut
Uses Driving, riding, jumping
Characteristics Strong and gentle

White blaze

Large head

Tail is set high

Strong, muscular legs

White stockings

HACKNEY HORSE

Hackneys are probably the world's best-known carriage horses. They were bred in England in the 18th and 19th centuries from the Yorkshire Roadster and the Norfolk Trotter, and were then crossed with Thoroughbreds. Hackney Horses are strong and have an elegant, high step. Before cars, Hackneys were used to pull carriages and were favoured for their grace. As a Hackney Horse moves, it throws its forelegs forward, keeping its knees high.

HEIGHT
14.2–16.2 hh

Hackneys have been developed as ponies as well as horses. They are one of few breeds that recognize both horse and pony sizes.

FACT FILE

Place of origin England

Colour Can be any colour, but mostly bay, chestnut or black

Uses Driving

Characteristics Sprightly and energetic

Well-shaped head is held high

Low withers

Tail is set high

Long neck

Compact body

Solid colour, often with white markings on legs

HANOVERIAN

Hanoverians have a noble history, having been bred from German and Thoroughbred horses for the Kings of England. Originally, these warmbloods were bred for riding, driving and for use on farms, but they were gradually developed to produce superb jumpers and performers in dressage. Hanoverians are often used, with great success, at Olympic events. These horses have steady personalities that are combined with a readiness to learn.

HEIGHT
15.2–16.2 hh

At the 2008 Olympics, Gold, Silver and Bronze medals in dressage all went to Hanoverians.

FACT FILE

Place of origin Germany

Colour Black, chestnut, bay, grey

Uses Jumping, dressage, showing

Characteristics Graceful and patient

High withers

Quarters are well-muscled

Athletic body

Body is deep through the girth

Strong limbs

IRISH DRAUGHT

Despite its name, the Irish Draught is a warmblood horse that is often used for cross-country racing and hunting. This breed was originally developed for heavy farm work as well as riding. Its ancestors were probably coldbloods mixed with Spanish horses, creating a strong horse with quick movement. The breed nearly died out several times in the past, but today, the Irish Draught is a popular horse.

HEIGHT
15.2–17 hh

Irish Draught horses are excellent jumpers. They are said to have 'hunters' feet' rather than the heavy hooves of their coldblood ancestors.

FACT FILE

Place of origin Ireland
Colour Any solid colour
Uses Showjumping, hunting, riding
Characteristics Strong and steady

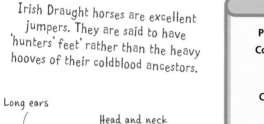

Long ears

Head and neck held high

Long back

Tail set high

Gentle expression

Very deep girth

Strong legs

Little or no feathering

LIPIZZANER

The Spanish Riding School in Austria is home to one of the most impressive horse breeds – **the Lipizzaner.** These fine riding horses were bred at a stud in Lipica, in Slovenia, 400 years ago. The aim was to develop the world's finest horses by breeding Spanish horses with other breeds, including Arabs. Lipizzaners are lively, have great grace and are fast to learn. They are trained to pull carriages and perform a huge range of movements, including leaps and advanced dressage.

HEIGHT
15.1–16.2 hh

This breed began with just six Spanish stallions that were bred with 24 mares. All of today's Lipizzaners are related to these six stallions.

FACT FILE

Place of origin Lipica, Slovenia

Colour Usually grey, but can be bay

Uses Riding, driving, dressage

Characteristics Intelligent and calm

Large eyes

Short, thick neck

Low withers

Strong hindquarters

Wide, deep chest

Powerful legs

Long body

MORGAN

T he Morgan – possibly the first breed to be developed in America – descended from a stallion called Justin Morgan. This original Morgan is thought to have been a mix of Arab and Thoroughbred and was named after its owner. The breed became famous for its abilities to work hard on the farm as well as for competing successfully in shows. Morgans are known for their gentle, affectionate natures.

HEIGHT
14.1–15.1 hh

Morgans have played an important role in developing many American breeds, including the Quarter Horse and the Tennessee Walking Horse.

FACT FILE

Place of origin Eastern USA

Colour Bay, brown, chestnut or black

Uses Riding, driving

Characteristics Intelligent and good-natured

Arab-like face

Arched neck holds head high

Rounded hindquarters

Tapering muzzle

Tail can be very long

Long, sloping shoulders

Long, compact body

Neat hooves

MUSTANG

Mustangs are tough, wild warmblood horses of the United States. They are descended from Spanish horses that were brought over by Europeans in the 16th century. By the 1900s there was a huge population of Mustangs roaming North America. People began hunting and killing the horses at an alarming rate and by the 1970s Mustangs had suffered a serious drop in numbers. Today, these wild horses are protected by law.

HEIGHT
13–16 hh

Due to interbreeding with other breeds, Mustangs can be almost any colour and they also vary a great deal in size. One Mustang reached 18 hands high.

FACT FILE

Place of origin Western USA

Colour Any colour, but brown, bay and chestnut are common

Uses Cattle herding

Characteristics Hardy and unpredictable

Can be any colour, with or without markings

Strong legs

Compact body

Hard hooves

PRZEWALSKI'S HORSE

These wild, sand-coloured horses were named by a Russian explorer called Nicolai Przewalski in the 1870s. Przewalski's Horses have existed in Europe and Asia for thousands of years. Their numbers dropped dramatically as people and other animals took over their habitat. This forced the wild herds to the edge of the Gobi desert, in Mongolia. Now the horses are protected in reserves where they are encouraged to breed.

HEIGHT
12–14.2 hh

There were around four primitive types of horse alive 10,000 years ago. Przewalski's Horse and the Tarpan are the only two that survive today.

FACT FILE

Place of origin Mongolia
Colour Dun with black points
Uses Wild
Characteristics Tough and sturdy

Eyes are set high on head

Points are black

Thick mane grows short and upright

Back may have an eel stripe

Short legs

Long body

Legs may have zebra stripes

QUARTER HORSE

Quarter Horses were first bred in the United States more than 300 years ago. During the week they were used for farm work and riding, and at the weekends they were ran in races. The races were conducted on a track a quarter of a mile (402 metres) long, which is how these horses got their name. Quarter Horses could outrun other breeds in these sprint races, reaching speeds of around 80 kilometres per hour. They are now bred for racing, cattle herding and use in rodeos.

HEIGHT
14–16 hh

Quarter Horses have been called the world's favourite horse — there are more than three million of them registered in the USA alone.

FACT FILE

Place of origin Virginia, USA

Colour Any solid colour

Uses Riding, cattle herding, racing, rodeo

Characteristics Agile and intelligent

Well-defined withers

Short, strong back and compact body

Muscular hindquarters

Short muzzle

Large nostrils

Deep, sloping shoulders

Forelegs are set wide

SELLE FRANCAIS

Selle Francais horses are also known as French Saddle Horses. It is an ancient breed that was originally developed in France, but English Thoroughbreds and other horses have been added to the mix. The result is a good, all-round horse with strength, intelligence, patience and an ability to learn. Selle Francais horses perform extremely well in showjumping and cross-country events, but they are also suited to general riding.

HEIGHT
15.2–17 hh

This breed is famous for its courage and willingness to tackle difficult fences.

FACT FILE

Place of origin Normandy, France

Colour Any, but chestnut is most common

Uses Jumping, eventing, riding

Characteristics Intelligent and brave

Neat head

Muscular hindquarters

Long neck

Deep chest

Sloping shoulders

Long body

SWEDISH WARMBLOOD

Crossing local Swedish horses with those
brought over from other parts of Europe
helped to develop the breed now known as the
Swedish Warmblood. These horses are elegant,
with the toughness of the small Swedish horses.
They are excellent competition horses and can
be trained to take part in many events. Swedish
Warmbloods compete at the Olympic Games,
but are as popular with amateur riders as they
are with professionals.

HEIGHT
16.2–17 hh

Swedish Warmbloods are rigorously
inspected to decide if they can
breed. This maintains the high
quality of the breed.

FACT FILE

Place of origin Sweden

Colour Any solid colour

Uses Riding, showjumping,
dressage, eventing

Characteristics Good-natured
and intelligent

Graceful
head

Long, elegant
neck

Powerful
hindquarters

Deep, strong
shoulders

Body is deep
through the girth

Well-formed hooves

TARPAN

The Tarpan originally lived in wild herds in central and eastern Europe and Russia. They were around for thousands of years before humans tamed them. However the breed became extinct in the 19th century. Since then breeders have attempted to recreate Tarpan horses by breeding other horses and ponies, such as the half-wild Konik horses from Poland.

HEIGHT
12.2–13.2 hh

The new breed of Tarpan is so similar to the old one that some people consider it to be almost the same as the extinct Tarpan.

FACT FILE

Place of origin Europe and Russia

Colour Dun

Uses Driving, riding

Characteristics Gentle and strong

Large head

Short mane

Black eel stripe

Short, thick neck

Legs may have zebra stripes

Dark hooves

TENNESSEE WALKER

Also called **Tennessee Walking Horses, this breed is said to have the sweetest nature of all warmbloods.** They enjoy being in the company of people and are good with children. Today, Tennessee Walkers are well known for their three extra gaits. In addition to the walk, trot and canter, these horses can perform the flat walk, the running walk and the rocking chair canter. All of them are smooth and comfortable for the rider.

HEIGHT
15–16 hh

Tennessee Walkers were developed by landowners who needed calm and patient horses to carry them around their large plantations.

FACT FILE

Place of origin Tennessee, USA
Colour Chestnut, black
Uses Riding, showing
Characteristics Lovely nature and sociable

In the USA, mane is clipped at the top of the neck

Arched neck

Short back

Large head with a straight profile

Broad chest

Strong, sloping shoulders

Strong legs

WALER

Walers get their names from the place they were first bred – New South Wales in Australia. They were used as working horses to carry their owners over large ranches where sheep and cattle were farmed. This breed is famous for its stamina – the horses can keep working for many hours before tiring. Walers have also been used in war, to carry soldiers and in police work.

HEIGHT
14.2–16 hh

Today, Walers are mostly used as general horses and in competitions, where their athletic abilities are put to good use.

FACT FILE

Place of origin New South Wales, Australia

Colour Any solid colour

Uses Riding, jumping

Characteristics Powerful and fast

Alert head

High withers

Strong hindquarters

Long neck

Deep girth

CASPIAN

The Caspian is often regarded as one of the oldest breeds of horse or pony, and may be an ancestor of the great Arab. There is evidence that these ponies have lived near the Caspian Sea, in what is now Iran, since prehistoric times. There are carvings and friezes from the Middle East dating to 3000 BC that depict these small ponies. Caspian ponies are used to pull carts and they also make good riding ponies for children.

HEIGHT
10–12 hh

This breed was rediscovered in the last century. Caspians are now being carefully bred in several countries to ensure their survival.

FACT FILE

Place of origin Iran
Colour All, but bay or chestnut are common
Uses Riding, showing, pulling
Characteristics Fast and strong

Short ears

Mane lies flat, as in Thoroughbreds

Body shape is more horse-like than pony-like

Fine, silky tail is set high

Small head

Long, arched neck

Narrow body

Slender legs without feathers

Small, oval-shaped hooves

CONNEMARA

These sturdy, yet gentle ponies are popular with both children and adults. Connemaras have lived in Ireland for hundreds of years and are thought to have a mixture of Spanish, Barb, Arab, Thoroughbred and Welsh Cob blood. They cope with the harsh weather conditions of the moors and are known for their hardiness. They have good jumping ability and are often used in hunts and shown in competitions.

HEIGHT
12.2–14.2 hh

Connemara is a region in Ireland. A group of local men formed the Connemara Pony Breeders Society, and in 1926 published the first Connemara pony stud book.

FACT FILE

Place of origin Ireland
Colour Grey, dun, chestnut, bay, roan, brown or black
Uses Riding, eventing
Characteristics Friendly and intelligent

Small ears

Well-arched neck

Short back

Powerful hindquarters

Long, thick tail

Compact head

Sloping shoulders

Short, strong legs

DALES

The Dales breed of pony has been around for 2000 years and was developed to carry heavy loads of metal from lead mines. Dales ponies worked in the hilly areas of northern England. They combine great strength with stamina and a willingness to work. Dales ponies are also comfortable riding ponies and they are quick to learn.

HEIGHT
Up to 14.2 hh

Dales ponies were originally bred from Clydesdale coldbloods and Welsh Cob ponies to produce these solid and dependable animals.

FACT FILE

Place of origin England
Colour Black, dark brown, bay
Uses Riding, driving
Characteristics Clever and strong

Neat head

Thick mane of long, straight hair

Powerful quarters

Deep and broad chest

Short legs with some feathering

DARTMOOR

Dartmoor ponies have survived on the moors of southwest England for at least **1000 years.** These animals are not pure-bred, but have been crossed with Thoroughbreds and Arabs to improve the breed. Dartmoors are also bred for use as childrens' riding ponies. They have gentle natures, making them suitable for children learning to ride and care for a pony.

HEIGHT
11.1–12.2 hh

Dartmoor ponies were bred at a prison in the 1900s, up until 1960. The guards used them to transport prisoners to and from jail.

FACT FILE

Place of origin England
Colour Bay, brown, black, chestnut, roan or grey
Uses Riding
Characteristics Strong and resilient

Small head

During winter, Dartmoor ponies grow thick coats

Muscular hindquarters

Low, sloping shoulders

Compact body

Hard hooves

EXMOOR

Exmoor ponies may be small, but they are tough and resilient. Their strength and hardiness comes from the harsh environment they have to endure. They are one of the world's oldest breeds, dating back to the Ice Age, and still survive as a free-living, wild herd on Exmoor. Tame Exmoors are bred as riding ponies and are used by disabled children, due to their gentle and reliable natures.

HEIGHT
12.2–12.3 hh

In the 1940s, Exmoor ponies nearly became extinct. Their numbers have increased since, but they are currently listed as an endangered breed of pony.

FACT FILE

Place of origin England
Colour Bay, brown or dun
Uses Riding
Characteristics Tough and hard-working

Light-coloured muzzle

Short ears

Broad, strong back

Points are black

Eye is hooded with a light-coloured ring around it (called a toad eye)

Short, strong legs

FALABELLA

The tiny Falabella is one of the world's smallest and rarest breeds. They are often called miniature horses because they have the proportions of a horse. Falabellas are the result of selective breeding. Over many years, only the smallest animals were chosen to breed, which encouraged smaller and smaller foals. However they are not very strong and can only be ridden by very young children.

HEIGHT
7–8.2 hh

Falabellas were first bred by the Falabella family of Argentina, by crossing a small Shetland pony with a small Thoroughbred horse.

FACT FILE

Place of origin Argentina
Colour Any
Uses Showing
Characteristics Friendly and intelligent

Head is slightly larger in proportion to body

Thick mane

Sleek coat

Low-set tail

Bay or black are the most common coat colours

Slim body

FELL

Fell ponies are one of the oldest native breeds and have played an important role in British history. Known for their sure-footedness, they were ideal for carrying loads on awkward routes. Because of this, they were often used by smugglers in Britain during the 17th and 18th centuries. They were also used on farms, to carry loads from mines and for riding. Today they are popular as family riding ponies and for driving, showing, trekking and hunting.

HEIGHT
13–14 hh

Fell pony numbers were declining 50 years ago. Now these ponies are one of Britain's most popular native breeds, although they still number less than 6000.

FACT FILE

Place of origin England
Colour Dark brown or black
Uses Riding, driving, trekking
Characteristics Hard-working and strong

Small, well-shaped head

Small ears

Long, full mane and tail

Square hindquarters

Large nostrils

Fine feather around heels

White markings are rare, but may occur as a star behind the fetlock

Well-formed hooves with slight blue colour

FJORD

Fjord ponies are an ancient breed that bear some primitive characteristics, also seen in **Przewalski's Horses.** These ponies get their name from the fjord regions in Norway where they originate from. They have been ridden and worked by people for 4000 years. Fjords have developed without cross-breeding, making them one of the purest breeds. They are known for their strength and have been used to pull loads and ploughs. Today they are used as riding ponies.

HEIGHT
13–14.2 hh

Fjords are pony-sized, but are often referred to as horses. They rarely grow taller than 14.2 hh — the top height limit for ponies.

FACT FILE

Place of origin Norway

Colour Dun

Uses Riding

Characteristics Calm and intelligent

Ears have dark tips

Thick mane is clipped so it stands upright

Mane contains a dark stripe

Dark dorsal stripe along pony's back

Coat is dun, but there are five varieties of shade

Arched neck

Smooth, sleek summer coat

Zebra stripes may be present on legs

Slight feathering on legs

HAFLINGER

These Austrian ponies were bred from native animals that were used on farms in the mountains. The modern breed was established in the 19th century from a stallion called Folie 249. Today, all Haflingers trace their ancestry back to this stallion. Haflingers have been transported around the world, becoming an international breed. They are friendly, calm ponies, making them popular with families.

HEIGHT
13–14.2 hh

Austrian Haflingers are branded on their left thigh with the letter 'H' and a symbol of the edelweiss — Austria's national flower.

FACT FILE

Place of origin Austria

Colour Chestnut, with flaxen or white mane and tail

Uses Driving, riding, trekking

Characteristics Long-lived and hardy

Large, expressive eyes

White or flaxen mane and tail

Chestnut coat

Well-shaped head

Stocky body

Strong legs and feet

HIGHLAND

The Highland is the largest of all native British ponies. The breed has been developed from wild ponies that lived in Scotland for thousands of years. They were bred to work on farms pulling ploughs and for forestry work, hauling timber. Highland ponies are well suited to cold weather – they are hardy in nature and grow thick winter coats. Modern Highlands have been mixed with Spanish horses and Thoroughbreds, producing ponies with calm natures.

HEIGHT
13–14.2 hh

There were once three types of Highland pony. Ponies from the Scottish islands were smaller than those from the mainland. Today there is just one breed.

FACT FILE

Place of origin Scotland
Colour Brown, black, dun or grey
Uses Riding, driving, trekking
Characteristics Hard-working and strong

Broad forehead

Long, thick mane and tail

Eel stripe is often present along back

Smooth summer coat, thick in winter

Large shoulders

Strong legs

Strong, muscular body

Zebra stripes may be present on legs

Feathering on legs

ICELANDIC

Icelandics are one of several breeds that may be regarded as either ponies or horses. They were first brought to Iceland in the first century AD by the invading Vikings. Later, a law was passed preventing any more horses or ponies being brought onto the island. This allowed a new, pure breed to develop. These ponies are extremely hardy from living outdoors in the freezing conditions of Iceland. Today, Icelandic ponies are used for riding, driving and in competitions.

HEIGHT
12.3–13.2 hh

Most horses and ponies move in four gaits: walk, trot, canter and gallop. Icelandics have two extra gaits known as running walk and flying pace.

FACT FILE

Place of origin Iceland

Colour Any

Uses Riding, driving, trekking

Characteristics Sure-footed and tough

Large head

Thick mane and tail

Sleek, shiny summer coat, thick in winter

Sloping hindquarters

Deep chest

Long, muscular body

Strong legs

51

NEW FOREST

This breed is one of the most adaptable of all ponies – New Forest ponies suit riding, jumping, hunting, dressage, cross-country, polo and much more! They respond well to people and are easy to ride. These ponies originally come from the woodlands of the New Forest in southern England, where they have lived for at least 1000 years. Around 100 years ago, the breed was improved by introducing Arab and Thoroughbred blood.

HEIGHT
12.2–14.2 hh

All New Forest ponies that roam wild have owners. Their owners are known as 'commoners' and they pay a small fee to leave their ponies in the woodland.

FACT FILE

Place of origin England

Colour Any, except piebald or skewbald

Uses Riding, dressage, hunting, showing

Characteristics Fast and friendly

Arched neck

Strong, muscular hindquarters

Short back

Large head

Sloping shoulders

Straight legs

Hard hooves

PONY OF THE AMERICAS

The Pony of the Americas, or POA, is a recently developed breed that came about when a Shetland pony was bred with an Arab/Appaloosa horse. The result was a strong, likeable pony with Appaloosa markings. These markings are patterned, often with dark spots and splashes on a pale-coloured coat, although there can be light markings on a dark coat.

HEIGHT
11.2–13 hh

The modern breed has been mixed with others to reduce the amount of Shetland pony blood and make the POA more horse-like.

FACT FILE

Place of origin Iowa, USA

Colour Appaloosa patterns (spots, speckles, frost, marble snowflake etc)

Uses Riding

Characteristics Calm and sweet-tempered

Large head with expressive eyes

Arched neck

Powerful hindquarters

Broad chest

Sloping shoulders

Short body

Appaloosa markings – spots may be oval or round

53

SHETLAND

Shetland ponies are hugely popular around the world. They are one of the world's smallest breeds, so can only be ridden by children. However Shetlands are strong and used for driving and pulling small carriages. These ponies originate from the Shetland Isles off the northeast coast of Scotland, where they have lived for thousands of years. The long, cold winters of this region have resulted in an extremely hardy breed.

HEIGHT
Up to 42 inches
(107 cm)

Shetlands are measured in inches, not hands. For a Shetland pony to be registered in the breed stud book, it should not exceed 42 inches in height.

FACT FILE

Place of origin Shetland Isles, Scotland

Colour Any

Uses Driving, riding, showing

Characteristics Strong and intelligent

Large eyes

Small ears

Sleek summer coat, thick in winter

Full tail

Neat head

Deep body

Short legs

WELSH SECTION B

The Welsh Section B, also known as the Welsh Pony, has Arab ancestors. It is thought that Welsh Mountain Ponies (Section A) were also bred with Hackneys and Thoroughbreds to create this modern breed. This produced an intelligent pony with long legs, making it ideal for riding. Welsh ponies move with elegance and have great agility. They often compete in gymkhanas and other competition events.

HEIGHT
12.2–13.2 hh

The four types of Welsh pony are Section A: Welsh Mountain Pony, Section B: Welsh Pony, Section C: Welsh Pony of Cob Type and Section D: Welsh Cob.

FACT FILE

Place of origin Wales

Colour Any

Uses Riding, eventing, showing

Characteristics Good-natured and strong

Attractive head

Long, arched neck

Light build

Large eyes

Body is deep through the girth

Long legs

55

GLOSSARY

Coldbloods Large, heavy horses from northern Europe, often used for pulling loads.

Colic Abdominal pain.

Conformation The shape and build of a horse or pony.

Deep through the girth A good measurement from the withers to the elbow. Desirable in conformation because it shows there is plenty of room for the lungs to expand.

Dressage The training of a horse or pony to develop obedience and to perform special movements.

Driving When horses or ponies are hitched up to vehicles, such as carts, and driven in shows and races.

Eel stripe A dark stripe, from the mane to the tail, along a horse's or pony's back.

Equid Any animal in the horse family.

Eventing A sport in which competitors take part in dressage, cross-country and showjumping over three days.

Feathers The long hair that grows on a horse's or pony's lower legs.

Foal A young horse or pony.

Gait The way a horse or pony moves.

Girth The strap that goes around a horse's or pony's belly to hold the saddle in place.

Gymkhana An event where horses and ponies, and their riders, take part in several competitions.

Hands high (hh) The unit that a horse's or pony's height is measured in. One hand is equal to 10 cm.

Herd A large group of animals that live together.

Hindquarters The back end of a horse or pony, including its hind legs.

Hotbloods Pure-bred, high-spirited horses, known for their speed.

Mare A female horse or pony, four years old or more.

Mitbah The angle at which the head meets the neck in Arabian horses.

Muzzle The area around a horse's or pony's mouth and nose.

Points of a horse The parts of a horse's or pony's anatomy.

Polo A team game played on horseback. Players score by hitting a small ball with a long-handled mallet into the opposing team's goal.

Show An event where horses or ponies are judged on their conformation and movement.

Stallion A male horse or pony, four years old or more.

Stamina The ability to sustain physical effort for a long time.

Stud book A book containing a list of all the registered pedigree animals of a breed.

Temperament The nature and behaviour of a horse or pony.

Turn out To let a horse or pony loose in a field or paddock.

Warmbloods Calm and sturdy horses that can run at speed.